THE BEATLES

" QUOTE UNQUOTE "

THE BEATLES

" QUOTE UNQUOTE "

Arthur Davis

ACKNOWLEDGEMENTS

The author and publisher acknowledge the following references, where
many of the quotes in this book can be found.

Roy Carr and **Tony Tyler**, *The Beatles — An Illustrated Record.* **Alan Clayson**, *The Quiet One — A Life of George Harrison.* **Alan Clayson**, *Ringo Starr — Straight Man or Joker?* **Hunter Davies**, *The Beatles.* **Chet Flippo**, *McCartney — The Biography.* **Geoffrey Giuliano**, *The Beatles — A Celebration.* **Andy Peebles**, *The Lennon Tapes.* **Neville Stannard**, *The Long and Winding Road.* **Neville Stannard**, *Working Class Heroes.* **Elizabeth Thomson** and **David Gutman** (eds), *The Lennon Companion.*

PICTURE CREDITS

© **Apple/Walter Shenson Films** pages 28, 35; © **Apple** page 55; **Camera Press, London** pages 2, 21; **Camera Press, London/Terence Spencer** pages 15, 19, 22, 25, 33, 40; **Camera Press, London/Frank Hermann** page 45; **Camera Press, London/David Nutter** page 50; **Camera Press, London/John Kelly** page 52; **Ronald Grant Archive** page 26; **Pictorial Press** back cover, pages 8, 16, 20, 24, 27, 31, 37, 38, 43, 46, 48, 49, 53, 56, 64; **Pictorial Press/Bob Gruen, Star File** page 69; **Pictorial Press/Terry McGough** page 76; **Range/Bettman/UPI** page 32; **Rex Features** front cover, pages 58, 71, 77, 79; **Rex Features/Fotex/H. Galuschka** page 62; **Rex Features/Richard Fitzgerald** page 67; **Rex Features/Brian Rasic** page 72; **Topham Picture Source** pages 6, 13; **Topham Picture Source/Press Association** page 11.

First published in Great Britain in 1994 by
Parragon Book Service Ltd
Units 13-17, Avonbridge Industrial Estate
Atlantic Road, Avonmouth
Bristol BS11 9QD

Publishing Manager: Sally Harper
Editor: Barbara Horn
Design and DTP: Crump Design

ISBN 1 85813 846 9

Printed in Italy

CONTENTS

OVERTURE

'Paul came round to my house one evening to look at the guitar manual I had, which I could never work out. We learned a couple of chords from it and managed to play "Don't You Rock Me, Daddy-O" with two chords.'

GEORGE

FACING PAGE: *Playing The Cavern club in Liverpool.*

THE STORY OF the most legendary group in the history of popular music began in Liverpool, a seaport in the north west of England, whose population, like many such places briefly visited by ships from all over the world for the purpose of unloading cargo and allowing passengers to disembark, was cosmopolitan. Records from the United States would find their way into local shops and then into the hands of young Liverpudlians besotted with rock 'n' roll, the blend of white country music and black rhythm and blues that had swept America in the mid-1950s and soon afterwards conquered Britain.

One such Liverpudlian teenager was John Lennon, born on 9 October 1940. His father, Fred Lennon, a steward on an ocean liner, spent longer away from his mother, Julia (after whom John titled a song on the 'double white album' in 1968), than with her. Because Julia's life was unsettled, John grew up living with Julia's sister, Mimi, and her husband, which gave his childhood the stability he otherwise might have missed. Despite this, the young John Lennon was disruptive at school, and seemed far more interested in listening to popular music than in getting an education. In 1956 John and several school chums formed a skiffle

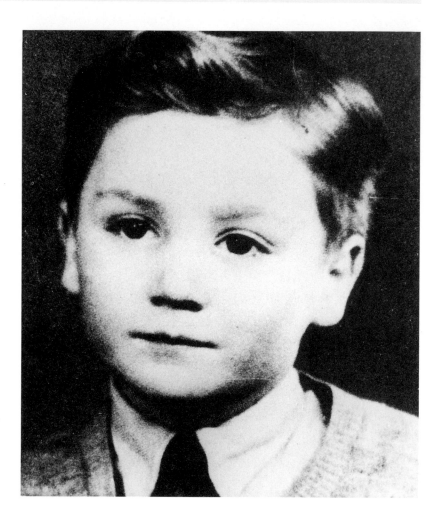

ABOVE: *The young John Lennon – butter wouldn't melt in his mouth.*

group, The Quarrymen, in the image of the group led by Britain's king of skiffle, Lonnie Donegan, whose 'Rock Island Line' had been a US Top Ten hit.

Paul McCartney, who was born on 18 June 1942, had a fairly normal upbringing. His mother, Mary McCartney, was a nurse, and his father, James, had once led a small-time jazz band. Mary McCartney tragically died of cancer in 1955. Like John, Paul also made reference to his mother – Mother Mary – in one of his songs ('Let It Be'). Paul was also smitten by rock 'n' roll, and taught himself to sing and play numerous contemporary hits by such heroes as Gene Vincent, Little Richard and Eddie Cochran after he acquired a guitar.

McCartney first encountered his future world-beating songwriting partner, John Lennon, in 1957, at a local church fête where The Quarrymen were playing. He joined eventually, and was a member in late 1957 when the group first played at The Cavern, a local jazz club, where they were instructed to restrict what they played to skiffle tunes rather than rock 'n' roll, which was not considered respectable by the jazz fraternity. In early 1958 McCartney introduced another guitarist, a young schoolfriend of his named George Harrison.

'A guitar's all right, John, but you'll never earn your living by it.' JOHN'S AUNT MIMI

'I'd never really been keen on the trumpet, but I liked the guitar because I could play it after just learning a few chords.' PAUL

> *'I first saw The Quarrymen when they were playing at the Wilson Hall at Garston. Paul was playing with them and said I should come and see them, and because I knew Paul, I got introduced to John. John said if I could play like this other guitarist, Eddie Clayton, I could join the group. I played them "Raunchy" and John said I could join. I was always playing "Raunchy" for them.'* GEORGE

Harrison was also mad for rock 'n' roll, and was encouraged by McCartney. George was showing considerable promise as a musician, and could play several instrumental hits of the day perfectly. He was accepted as a member of the group without delay.

During 1958, when John was at art college, his mother was accidentally killed by a car. John was clearly distraught at the loss, although he contrived to cover up his grief with alcoholic excess.

The Quarrymen continued as before, with Lennon, McCartney and Harrison (all singer/guitarists) joined by other young musicians, most of whom stayed only a short time. In late 1959 the group played in a talent contest held in Manchester, for which they used the name of Johnny & The Moondogs. They didn't come close to winning, perhaps because the other group members did not share the future Beatle trio's commitment.

In early 1960 they acquired a bass player, Stuart Sutcliffe, who was John's best friend at art college, and a talented painter. Sutcliffe impressed Lennon because he was a leader rather than a follower. He and Lennon would 'hang out' in a local coffee bar, the Jacaranda, which was run by local entrepreneur Allan Williams, who became the group's first manager. During this period, London agent and promoter Larry Parnes, who managed many British rock stars of the time, asked Williams to nominate four Liverpool groups who could back his 'stars' on tours in the north of England and Scotland. Hardly surprisingly, one of the groups Williams recommended was Johnny & The Moondogs, although he advised them that they urgently needed to change the group name. As they were all great admirers of the Texan rock 'n' roll star, Buddy Holly – Paul McCartney would

LEFT: *George Harrison (left), John Lennon (right) and Stuart Sutcliffe (centre), photographed by Astrid Kirchherr.*

later purchase the music publishing rights to the vast majority of Holly's catalogue of songs – they adopted a similar approach to choosing a new group name as Holly had when he changed the name of the group he led from The Three Tunes to The Crickets. After considering and rejecting the names of other insects, someone suggested The Beetles, and Lennon swiftly amended the spelling of the name to Beatles, reflecting the then current terminology which regarded them as a 'beat' group.

The group made a brief tour of Scotland backing Johnny Gentle, one of the lesser artists in the Parnes stable. The foursome returned to Liverpool having failed to make any real progress, but realizing the need to have a drummer in the group. They had often played at a club known as The Casbah in the cellar of a private house owned by Mrs Mona Best, whose son, Pete, was a drummer, and by the summer of 1960 he had joined the group. At the same time Allan Williams met the owner of a club in Hamburg who had already hired one band from Liverpool, Derry Wilkie and The Seniors. Because that group had been popular with his customers, he wanted another. Williams was concerned that The Beatles, whom he still regarded as untried, might

disgrace him, but when both Rory Storm & The Hurricanes and Gerry & The Pacemakers (who would later rival The Beatles as the premier Liverpool group) turned down his offer, he was left with little option and had to nominate The Beatles. Less than a week after he joined The Beatles, Pete Best and his new colleagues crossed the channel on a ferry on their way to Hamburg. The Indra Club, where they would be playing, was small and rather dirty, and their communal living quarters were a single sparsely furnished room situated directly behind the screen of a cinema, the Bambi Kino, which was in use whenever the club (which was in the same building) was closed.

They were all young enough to survive in these conditions on limited amounts of sleep, despite often performing in the club for up to six hours a night. On that first trip to Hamburg, which lasted three months, The Beatles played over one hundred shows, first at the Indra and later at the larger Kaiserkeller.

Because their repertoire was extremely limited (to around thirty songs), the group found it necessary not only to repeat some songs several times during each night's show, but also to artificially extend them by

RIGHT: *Ringo Starr played with Rory Storm & The Hurricanes before joining The Beatles.*

incorporating lengthy instrumental solos. While this may have initially made their performances seem unprofessional, ultimately it instilled in them the knowledge that their job was to entertain. This also involved movement around the stage, and in Lennon's case, sometimes rolling on the floor while still playing his guitar.

Towards the end of their stay, Lennon, McCartney and Harrison met the man who would become the final member of the group that would conquer the world three years later. Rory Storm & The Hurricanes, who had turned down the residency that was accepted by The Beatles, had later changed their minds, and were also playing in the Hamburg clubs. The group's guitarist, Wally Egmond, used The Beatles as his backing group in a local studio when he recorded a version of George Gershwin's 'Summertime'. On that occasion the Hurricanes' drummer, Richard Starkey (who acquired his nickname, Ringo Starr, because of the large number of rings on his fingers) played rather than Pete Best. Starkey, born 7 July 1940, didn't immediately join the other three quarters of the 'Fab Four' (as they were eventually dubbed), but the initial vital contact had been made.

'I always felt I'd make it. There were some moments of doubt, but I knew something would eventually happen. When Mimi used to throw away things I'd written or drawn, I used to say "You'll regret that when I'm famous", and I meant it.' JOHN

FACING PAGE: *The Beatles at the height of their popularity, photographed by Terence Spencer.*

STAR CLUB TO STAR TURN

'We probably loved the Cavern best of anything. We never lost our identification with the audience all the time. We never rehearsed anything, not like the other groups who kept on copying The Shadows.' GEORGE

FACING PAGE: *Bill Harry, editor of* MERSEYBEAT *(Liverpool's local music magazine), presents the magazine's award to The Beatles in 1962.*

ON THEIR RETURN from Germany in late 1960, The Beatles surprised audiences in Liverpool with their evident improvement as musicians. They came back without Stuart Sutcliffe, who had become romantically involved with Astrid Kirchherr, a striking blonde German woman. Astrid, an innovative photographer, and Stu, a promising painter, were drawn together and quickly became engaged. She restyled her fiancé's hair and John, Paul and George soon adopted a similar hairstyle, which would become the familiar Beatle look in 1963. Astrid also designed stage clothes for the group, although Pete Best preferred to retain his Teddy-boy looks.

The Beatles had not left Hamburg voluntarily. Having achieved the status of one of the city's emergent groups, they had been invited to play at a rival venue, the newly opened Top Ten club. In retaliation, the Kaiserkeller's manager had alerted authorities to the fact that George Harrison was not yet eighteen, and was thus legally barred from nightclubs after midnight. Until George reached that age, on 25 February 1961, it would be foolish for The Beatles to return. However, it did not mean that the group was at a loose end, as in the meantime the management of The Cavern had introduced the concept of shows at lunchtime, and from early 1961 The Beatles were a regular attraction there.

In April 1961 The Beatles were back in Hamburg for another three-month residency, this time at the Top Ten Club. During this visit, they finally lost Sutcliffe, who had been offered a place at a German art college. He had been invited to live with Astrid's parents and decided to give up his musical career, which was not, after all, his forte. The combination of circumstances left Lennon with no option but to allow McCartney to become the group's bass player – after all, three guitarists were unnecessary, and the change would probably improve the group's sound.

During this residency The Beatles made their first record ever to be released, which indirectly led to their meeting Brian Epstein, who became their manager, and played a considerable part in their success story. In fact, The Beatles were neither the stars of their first record, nor was their name used on its label. The featured artist was a British singer/guitarist named Tony Sheridan, who was also appearing at the Top Ten club and was spotted by German record producer Bert Kaempfert, an orchestra leader whose 'Wonderland by Night' had

FACING PAGE: *The distinctive Beatle look was based on a hairstyle created for Stuart Sutcliffe by Astrid Kirchherr.*

topped the American singles chart earlier that year. Sheridan decided to use The Beatles as his backing group, but when the single came out with beat-group versions of 'My Bonnie Lies Over The Ocean' and 'When The Saints Go Marching In', the record label credited Tony Sheridan and The Beat Brothers, as Kaempfert felt this was more appropriate. At the end of the recording session The Beatles were allowed to record a couple of tracks on their own. Lennon took the lead vocal on a 'rocked-up' cover version of the pre-war music-hall favourite 'Ain't She Sweet', while the other track was 'Cry For A Shadow', an instrumental tribute to/parody of the sound of The Shadows, the foremost British group in the early 1960s, when solo vocalists dominated the charts.

When The Beatles had completed their Hamburg stint in mid-1961, they returned once more to Liverpool and the Cavern. Lennon helped a friend of his from art college, Bill Harry, to publish a magazine about the local music scene, *Mersey Beat* (Liverpool stands on the River Mersey). One of the places that sold the magazine was North End Music stores, a record shop owned by a wealthy local family, the Epsteins, and managed by their well-educated son, Brian, who

LEFT: *John Lennon strikes a pose in a TV studio dressing room in Birmingham, England, in 1963.*

LEFT: *Eventually, Brian Epstein gave up his job running his family's record store to manage The Beatles.*

had previously failed to settle in several careers. The record shop had given Brian an interest in music, and he prided himself on being able to find any record a customer might ask to buy. On 28 October 1961, one Raymond Jones asked for a single on which a local group known as The Beatles were playing. Although *Mersey Beat,* in which the group were strongly featured, was stocked in his shop, Epstein possibly hadn't read it, as he was not a pop music aficionado, and apparently he was unaware that this local quartet played most lunchtimes at the Cavern, a few hundred metres from his shop. When he found out, he went to the venue to ask the group which label had released the single. He ordered a large quantity (around two hundred), which sold well. Before long, Epstein was managing The Beatles, and trying to use his limited influence as a prominent retailer to find them a recording contract. He managed to convince Decca Records, at the time one of the two major labels in Britain, to grant

them an audition, and on the first day of 1962 they arrived in London and were rejected in favour of Brian Poole & The Tremeloes, a group from Dagenham in Essex, not far from London.

Epstein played the audition tape to other labels, but without success, and in April 1962, the group returned to Germany. While The Beatles played for seven weeks at the Star Club in Hamburg, Epstein found them a record label. He had been recommended to record producer George Martin, who was running the small Parlophone label, owned by the giant EMI record company. Soon after their return from the Continent, the group was signed by Martin, who recommended that they change their drummer. For many groups, this would have been a difficult problem involving loyalty, but Pete Best's three colleagues were eventually persuaded by Epstein that Best, who was somewhat of a loner anyway, should be replaced. The group chose Ringo Starr as their new drummer, and he joined in August 1962.

Less than three weeks later, Starr was in EMI's Abbey Road studios with his new colleagues, although George Martin had also hired a session musician to play drums in case Ringo was no better than Best, which

'I didn't like the look of Rory's drummer myself. He looked the nasty one, with his little grey streak of hair. But the nasty one turned out to be Ringo, the nicest of them all.' GEORGE

'I was nervous and terrified of the studio. When we came back to do the B-side of "Love Me Do", I found that George Martin had this other drummer sitting in my place. It was terrible — I'd been asked to join The Beatles, but now it looked as if I was only going to be good enough to do ballrooms with them, but not good enough for records.' RINGO

RIGHT: *George Harrison
and Ringo Starr arriving
at the Empire Theatre in
Liverpool.*

RIGHT: *In concert at the end of 1963. With his sunglasses, John appears to have been the first of the group to change from performer to rock star.*

didn't help the newcomer a bit. George Harrison was also nervous, as can be judged from his response to George Martin asking the group in the studio whether there was anything they didn't like: 'For a start, I don't like your tie.' Also during that three weeks Lennon married Cynthia Powell, with whom he had had a steady relationship since 1958 and who was now pregnant. The news was suppressed at the time to prevent female fans turning against The Beatles.

The Beatles' first single released under their own name was 'Love Me Do', a Lennon/McCartney composition, which briefly reached the UK Top Twenty, but was not released outside Britain at the time. Two more trips to Hamburg before the end of 1962 found The Beatles gaining in confidence and ability. Between the two visits, they returned to Abbey Road to record a follow-up to their first hit, another Lennon/McCartney song, 'Please Please Me', which was released in January 1963, and was their first major success, topping three of the four British charts and reaching Number Two in the fourth, as the group became incredibly popular in a short time due to constant touring. However, they put down their collective foot and made it clear that they preferred to release one of their

'Touring was a relief, just to get out of Liverpool and break new ground. We were beginning to feel stale and cramped. We'd outlived the Hamburg stage and wanted to pack that up. We hated going back to Hamburg those last two times. We'd had all that scene.' JOHN

own songs rather than one they had unenthusiastically recorded at the same session – 'How Do You Do It'. The rejected song was given to another Liverpool group whom Martin was producing, Gerry & the Pacemakers. In February 1963 The Beatles recorded another ten tracks in one day, which became the basis of their debut LP, *Please Please Me,* and included both sides of each of their first two singles. The LP was certain to do well, as a week before it appeared the group's third single, 'From Me To You', had topped the UK singles chart.

The Beatles could do no wrong, it seemed, and in August 1963 'She Loves You', another Number One single, maintained momentum, while *Please Please Me* dominated the British LP chart, remaining at the top for over seven months. Britain was conquered, but the rest of the world, and especially the United States, was thus far showing no sign of similar capitulation.

RIGHT: *On a British pop show during the 1960s. Helen Shapiro is on Ringo's right.*

'In order to consolidate their success, I had to have an album on the market very quickly, and the thing to do was record as many numbers as I could from their existing repertoire.'

GEORGE MARTIN, ON THE SIX COVER VERSIONS ON *PLEASE PLEASE ME*.

YOU MAY TELEPHONE
FROM HERE

TOP OF THE POPS

'I get my spasms of being intellectual. I read about politics, but I don't think I'd vote for anyone — no messages from any phoney politicians are coming through me.'

JOHN

By mid-1963 Britain was gripped with a phenomenon known as Beatlemania. All over the country teenage boys adopted Beatle hairstyles (actually a non-style, which led to the group being known as mop-tops) and treated every utterance by members of the group as either inspirational wisdom or God-like philosophy, neither of which had any basis in fact, as both John Lennon and Paul McCartney separately confirmed. However, whether they liked it or not, The Beatles were elevated to the status of icons, especially after their appearance at the Royal Variety Performance in November that year. Later that month a second LP, *With The Beatles,* finally ended the thirty-week chart-topping run of *Please Please Me.*

With The Beatles remained at Number One for twenty-one weeks, by which time the group's influence had spread across the Atlantic Ocean. Despite their huge success in Britain, Capitol Records, the label that had the contractual rights to their records in the United States, had thus far declined to release them. This allowed smaller independent labels to license the records for the American market, although none of them reached the chart in 1963. However, in early 1964 Capitol decided to finally exer-

cise their option, to coincide with the band making their first visit to America, where they were booked to play live on television on the nationally networked *Ed Sullivan Show.* The audience that watched the group on Sullivan's show was estimated at 70 million! The handful of live concerts played by The Beatles on this trip immediately sold out, as 'I Want To Hold Your Hand', their

---

'I don't feel like I imagine an idol is supposed to feel.' PAUL

---

fifth British hit single (which had inevitably reached Number One as soon as it was released), also became their first American hit, topping the US chart two weeks after release. This started an avalanche of chart activity that has never been equalled, as every Beatle record previously released in America suddenly entered the US chart to provide the greatest chart domination ever, with twelve singles simultaneously in the US Top 100, five of them in the top five places,

LEFT: *In Washington on their first American tour in 1964.*

'During the next number, the ones in the cheap seats, clap your hands, and the rest of you just rattle your jewellery.'

JOHN AT THE ROYAL VARIETY PERFORMANCE

and two LPs in the top two places in the album chart. Even 'My Bonnie', the single on which they had backed Tony Sheridan, spent six weeks in the US chart.

Many of these US hits had appeared in Britain only as LP tracks or B-sides, but eventually 'I Want To Hold Your Hand' (No. 1), 'She Loves You' (No. 1), 'Please Please Me', 'Twist and Shout', 'Do You Want To Know A Secret' and 'Love Me Do' (No. 1) all reached the top three of the US chart, as did the group's newest British single, 'Can't Buy Me Love'.

It took hardly any time before talk began of The Beatles appearing in a film, and on their return from their first American visit, the group began work on their first feature movie, *A Hard Day's Night*. Because United

RIGHT: *Small guitar, big success — John seemed always ready to pose for the cameras.*

Artists, who commissioned the work, were still unsure of the commercial potential of a film starring The Beatles, *A Hard Day's Night* (titled after a phrase coined by Ringo after a lengthy period of filming) was shot in black and white and involved little more than the quartet being themselves. The film also included six new Lennon/McCartney songs as well as 'Can't Buy Me Love', which had sold over 1.2 million copies in its first week on release in Britain, and over 2 million in its first week in the United States.

During the filming, George Harrison met his future wife, model Patti Boyd, who had a part in the movie. Before the film was premiered in July, several other newsworthy items had taken place: in March Lennon's book of poetry, *In His Own Write,* had been published, and he had been guest of honour at a literary function celebrating the four-hundredth anniversary of Shakespeare's birth; *Newsweek* magazine in America dubbed him 'an unlikely heir to the English tradition of literary nonsense'. At the end of May life-size models of the group appeared in London's world-famous Madame Tussaud's wax museum. A few days later Ringo was rushed to hospital with tonsillitis and was replaced for the first dates of the group's first world tour by Jimmy Nicol.

During that summer The Beatles again made history when both the single and album of *A Hard Day's Night* topped the US and UK charts simultaneously in the week of 4 August. At the end of an incredible year Ringo was back in hospital to have his tonsils removed; afterwards, when asked to tell reporters how he was, he was able to say 'I feel fine' – appropriate, as this was the title of the group's new single, which was an immediate international smash hit. The end of the year brought a fourth LP, *Beatles For Sale,* following the soundtrack album of *A Hard Day's Night,* which had inevitably topped the charts all over the world, not least because the film had received considerable acclaim. *Beatles For Sale* was similarly successful, and included cover versions of classic songs from the rock 'n' roll era by Chuck Berry ('Rock 'n' Roll Music'), Buddy Holly ('Words Of Love') and Carl Perkins ('Honey Don't', with Ringo as lead vocalist, and 'Everybody's Trying To Be My Baby', with George as featured singer). It was a worthy end to an amazing year for The Beatles, which had brought the group no less than thirty hit singles in the United States, an incredible achievement.

As their film, *A Hard Day's Night,* had been a worldwide success, reputedly

LEFT: *A still from* HELP!, *which premiered during the summer of 1965.*

earning many millions of dollars on its initial release, everyone was anxious for The Beatles to make another movie. In early 1965 they began work on *Help!*, which was originally to be called *Eight Arms To Hold You*. Before it was premiered during the summer of 1965, there was another chart-topping single, 'Ticket To Ride', with McCartney playing guitar. This song later became the first (minor) hit for American brother and sister duo The Carpenters, but the original hit single by The Beatles was somewhat overshadowed by 'Help!', which – like 'A Hard Day's Night' – topped the British and American singles and album charts, although not simultaneously this time. Shortly before *Help!* was premiered, it was announced that The Beatles had been awarded the MBE (Member of the British Empire) in Queen Elizabeth II's birthday honours list, which provoked complaints from some other recipients of the medal, some of whom, representatives of the older generation, returned their medals, something that John Lennon would do a few years later, although for very different reasons.

Before they actually received their decorations from the Queen at Buckingham Palace, the group had embarked on another

'The British house of royalty has put me on the same level as a bunch of vulgar numskulls.'
A HOLDER OF THE MBE, WHEN THE AWARD TO THE BEATLES WAS ANNOUNCED

'We thought being offered the MBE was as funny as everybody else thought it was. Why? What for? We all met and agreed it was daft. It all just seemed part of the game we'd agreed to play, like getting the Ivor Novello Awards. We agreed in order to annoy even more people who were already annoyed.' JOHN

RIGHT: *The Beatles show off their new MBEs in June 1965.*

'There was only one person in the United States that
we really wanted to meet.' JOHN ON MEETING ELVIS

RIGHT: *As respectable a
pop group as one could
wish to see (to modern
eyes), The Beatles still
enjoyed a joke in front of a
mirror.*

world tour. During that trip to California the group also achieved a lifetime ambition by meeting one of their earliest and greatest heroes, Elvis Presley, for the first and only time, at his house in Bel Air.

1965 was yet another action-packed year for the group. Ringo Starr and his girlfriend, Maureen Cox, were married in February and produced a son, Zak, by Christmas, and John Lennon's second book, *A Spaniard in the Works,* was published and received as much praise as *In His Own Write.* However, the most enduring Beatle-related item of the year was a track included on the *Help!* LP, although it was not featured in the movie. Written by Paul McCartney, 'Yesterday' was recorded without participation from any of the other members of the group – Paul sang to his own guitar accompaniment, and was backed by a string quartet. The track was released as a single in the United States, where it topped the chart for a month and sold a million copies. It was first released as a single in Britain in 1976, when it reached the Top Ten, despite already being owned by the millions who had bought the *Help!* album. Credited to Lennon/McCartney (as were all compositions written by either or both during the life of The Beatles, even when, as in this case, one of the team had little or nothing to do with it), 'Yesterday' is the Beatle composition that has been recorded by more acts than any other, an estimated 2,500, and was also the first ever song to be performed over five million times on radio and television in the United States, yet another remarkable achievement.

'None of us ever worried about things like the future. I've always just taken chances myself and been lucky. I've always had a few bob in my pocket. There were good and bad nights on the tours, but they were really all the same. The only fun part was the hotels in the evening, smoking pot and that.' RINGO

THE PEAK

'We couldn't say it, but we didn't really like going back to Liverpool. Being local heroes made us nervous, and when we did shows there, they were always full of people we knew. We felt embarrassed in our suits and being very clean, because we were worried that friends might think we'd sold out — which we had, in a way.'

JOHN

THE END OF 1965 brought another new LP, *Rubber Soul,* which the group were obliged to deliver to EMI under their contract which demanded two albums a year. On the same day that *Rubber Soul* appeared – 3 December 1965 – so did another new single, 'We Can Work It Out'/'Day Tripper', which swiftly topped charts around the world, heralding the LP's imminent arrival at the top of the album lists. Although no-one knew it at the time, the end of the year brought the final British tour by The Beatles, including their last show on Merseyside.

The following year began with George marrying Patti Boyd, but there was no doubt that the most significant event of the first half of the year was a John Lennon interview in a London newspaper in which he told Maureen Cleave that Christianity would not last for ever. No-one in Britain took much notice but his flippant remarks would bring the group a lot of grief before long. In June the second single of the year, 'Paperback Writer', provided no clue that a potential storm was brewing, topping the charts everywhere (although it was the first Beatles single since 'She Loves You' to enter the British chart as low as Number Two!). Things started going ominously wrong in early July during a two day visit to the Philippines as part of what would be The Beatles' final world tour, and the group were fortunate to escape shaken but not injured from an angry crowd who felt they had deeply insulted President Marcos.

At the end of the same month an American magazine published the Lennon interview with Maureen Cleave and, within two days of its appearance, the skies across North America were illuminated by public bonfires of records by the blasphemous Beatles. This was a serious problem, which continued to escalate until John made a public apology on American television, after which the group were able to continue with what would be their final live dates in the United States.

Just as that final American tour began, a new album, *Revolver,* was released, as well as another major new single, 'Eleanor

---

'Christianity will go, it will vanish and shrink. I needn't argue about that, I'm right and I will be proved right.' JOHN TO MAUREEN CLEAVE

Rigby' / 'Yellow Submarine'. It was clear that the pressures of success were starting to take their toll, as the tracks on the single were also included on the LP, something that previously had been avoided in Britain, and *Revolver* was also the group's only new album of the year. Both songs on the single quickly became great favourites, 'Eleanor Rigby' for McCartney's wistful lyrics about loneliness and for its use of a string quartet, and 'Yellow Submarine', with lead vocals by Ringo, for its sing-along qualities. *Revolver* was the start of a stylistic change, somewhat away from pure pop songs (although some were in evidence, as another harvest of cover versions proved, even if the only one that became a hit was Cliff Bennett's 'Got To Get You Into My Life') and towards the

'It was terrible. They hurt because they don't have soft jelly babies in America, but hard jelly beans like bullets. Some newspaper had dug out the old joke which we'd forgotten about, when John once said I'd eaten all his jelly babies, and everywhere we went, I got them thrown at me.'

GEORGE, ON THE DANGERS OF TOURING IN THE US

'Touring was dangerous sometimes, but we never thought about it. A plane did catch fire once in Texas and scared everyone, and once we flew from Liverpool to London with a window open. We were a bit worried when our death was predicted on a plane in the States — that wasn't nice.'

RINGO

then fashionable psychedelic style pioneered by such Californian acts as Jefferson Airplane and Country Joe & The Fish. The track on *Revolver* most obviously of this persuasion was 'Tomorrow Never Knows', on which Lennon's vocal was distorted.

On their return to Britain, John, Paul and George worked separately on projects that did not involve any of their colleagues. John appeared in a black comedy film, *How I Won The War,* in the non-musical role of Private Gripweed, while George went to India to study the subcontinent's music and culture, and Paul wrote the score for *The Family Way,* a film starring Hayley Mills. These diverse activities led to rumours that the group were disbanding. These stories were emphatically denied by McCartney.

In November 1966 John Lennon met the Japanese avant-garde artist Yoko Ono when he attended an exhibition of her work at a London art gallery, just before The Beatles began work on what would be acclaimed as their finest album.

The new year, 1967, started with EMI signing the group for another nine years, as George Martin supervised sessions for a new album. The first new single of the year caused a considerable stir — the titles of both 'Penny Lane' and 'Strawberry Fields

FACING PAGE: *John Lennon sits with George Martin at the Abbey Road studios in London, during the recording of* SERGEANT PEPPER'S LONELY HEARTS CLUB BAND.

'The rumour we were splitting up was rubbish, because we're all great friends and we don't want to split up. There's never been any talk of it — except by other people.' PAUL

Forever' referred to actual places in Liverpool, and the tracks were so different from the group's early work that this was the group's first single in four years that failed to top the British chart, unable to dislodge the schmaltzy 'Release Me' by Engelbert Humperdinck. In the United States, 'Penny Lane' topped the singles chart to become the group's thirteenth Number One in three years, while 'Strawberry Fields' separately reached the Top Ten. But this was only the *hors-d'oeuvres:* in June the world was amazed by the LP that had been recorded during the same sessions, *Sergeant Pepper's Lonely Hearts Club Band*, still widely regarded as the finest album ever released.

The idea was McCartney's — The Beatles would play the parts of the band in a variety show, with Ringo, for example, as Billy

RIGHT: *The Beatles at the launch of the SERGEANT PEPPER'S LONELY HEARTS CLUB BAND album.*

Shears, singing 'With A Little Help From My Friends', one of a number of songs on the album that would become world-famous. Others included 'Lucy In The Sky With Diamonds' (assumed by many to be about the drug LSD, but which its writer, John Lennon, always maintained was inspired by a painting by his young son, Julian); McCartney's 'She's Leaving Home' and 'When I'm 64', and the final track, 'A Day In The Life' (which was banned by the BBC because of a line including the words 'turn you on', which were assumed to be about taking drugs). The album sleeve was also sensational; a collage, in the style of a school photograph, of sixty-eight people (including The Beatles themselves, both in person and as waxworks) who the group regarded as influential, including comedians such as Laurel and Hardy and W.C. Fields, film stars (Fred Astaire, Marilyn Monroe), sportsmen (boxer Sonny Liston, Liverpool footballer Albert Stubbins), novelists, poets, painters and so on. Later that month the group was involved in an equally world-shattering event: for the first live satellite TV broadcast, The Beatles were invited to play a previously unheard song for an estimated global audience of 400 million people. They actually sang live to an instrumental backing track recorded a few hours earlier, but the broadcast was a sensation; viewers all over the world simultaneously heard 'All You Need Is Love', a most appropriate song for the period that became known as the Summer of Love.

Then things started going wrong again. The group had collectively decided that the study of transcendental meditation as practised by the Indian guru, Maharishi Mahesh Yogi was worthy of investigation, and all attended a ten-day course in Wales. While they were away, Brian Epstein, who was concerned that the group might not renew his management contract when it expired in October 1967, was found dead at his London flat, apparently from an accidental overdose of sleeping pills.

'You know when they turn over the last page of one section to show you it's come to an end before going on to the next part? That was what Brian's death was like, the end of a chapter.'

GEORGE, ON THE DEATH OF BRIAN EPSTEIN

ABOVE: 'All You Need Is
Love' became the anthem
for 1967's Summer of
Love.

The quartet now made one of their few professional mistakes: they presumed that they could direct a TV special. McCartney had conceived the idea of *Magical Mystery Tour*, in which the group would be filmed as they were driven around Britain in a chara-banc with a number of actors and hangers-on. The plan was to film the journey, during which the group would perform half a dozen new songs. The completed show was

BELOW: With Brian Epstein's death, The Beatles lost their greatest supporter. Despite the group's continued popularity, things were no longer the way they had been.

'*Now that we only play in the studios and not anywhere else, we haven't got a clue about what we're going to do. We have to start from scratch, thrashing it out in the studio, doing it the hard way. If Paul has written a song, he comes into the studio with it in his head.*' GEORGE

filmed in colour (although the vast majority of TV sets in Britain could show only black-and-white pictures), and was premiered on 26 December 1967, on a just-launched TV channel with a limited audience. It was deservedly panned as barely comprehensible self-indulgence, but its one redeeming feature was the music, released as a double EP packaged with a twenty-four-page booklet. One of the notable new songs was 'I Am The Walrus', which was also used as the B-side of 'Hello Goodbye', which instantly topped the world's singles charts and was the group's final single of a dramatic year which had produced triumph and tragedy in virtually equal measures.

DECLINE...

'We knew from the beginning of MAGICAL MYSTERY TOUR that we were just practising. We knew we weren't taking time or doing things properly, but when you've spent a long time on something, even when it's not good enough, you begin to feel that perhaps it's better than you know it is. I'm glad it was badly received. It would have been bad to get away with it, and now it's a challenge to do something properly.' PAUL

FACING PAGE: *John Lennon and Yoko Ono flew to Gibraltar for their wedding in March 1969.*

Somewhat bruised by the hostile critical reception of *Magical Mystery Tour,* The Beatles nevertheless brushed aside criticism: bad reviews could not affect their supreme self-confidence. In early 1968, The Beatles announced the launch of Apple Corps Ltd, a company that would become the administrative and creative centre of many new enterprises involving the group, individually and collectively. One of its first undertakings was the Apple boutique on Baker Street in London's West End, with much of the fashionably far-out clothing sold there designed by a group of Dutch hippies known as The Fool. While the shop, with its garish psychedelic exterior, quickly became popular both as a landmark and an eyesore, the *laissez-faire* attitude of its staff to security meant that large quantities of merchandise were stolen; after eight chaotic months, the shop was closed and the remaining stock given away. Some aspects of the Apple empire were more enduring, such as Apple Records, but others, like Apple Tailoring and Apple Electronics, were as short-lived as the boutique.

In February 1968, the four Beatles, with their wives and lovers, made a pilgrimage to India to visit the Maharishi for a scheduled three-month visit. Ringo and Maureen

Left: *Paul McCartney with Jane Asher; their engagement ended after Paul met photographer Linda Eastman.*

returned home after ten days and Paul and Jane Asher followed them after six weeks. This was a somewhat unrewarding visit for The Beatles, but the release of a new single, 'Lady Madonna', which topped the UK chart but only reached the US Top Five, diverted attention from their absence. Soon after their return from India, both John

Lennon and Paul McCartney would begin new romantic relationships, Lennon after spending the night romancing Yoko Ono (during which they recorded *Two Virgins,* an experimental LP), which led to Cynthia divorcing him, and McCartney announcing that his engagement to actress Jane Asher had ended, shortly after he met American photographer Linda Eastman.

Before a new (and brilliant) single was released, an animated feature film, *Yellow Submarine,* was premiered, with music by The Beatles, although the film's soundtrack album was delayed to allow the release of a new Beatles studio album, the follow-up to *Sergeant Pepper.* 'Hey Jude', the new single, was the first by the group to bear the Apple label, and was also their longest, lasting over seven minutes. After two weeks at the top of the British chart, it was replaced at Number One by a second Apple hit, 'Those Were The Days', sung by Mary Hopkin. This auspicious start for Apple Records was unfortunately not sustained, as other performers signed to the label mostly failed to achieve similar success during their time associated with Apple.

The label was yet another example of the quartet's belief that whatever they attempted would be successful, which many began

to doubt after they heard the 1968 double album simply titled *The Beatles,* which came in a plain white sleeve. Over-confidence was blamed for what seemed an overlong collection of 30 tracks, several of which seemed hastily assembled, although none provoked such a negative reaction as 'Revolution 9', an unlistenable collage of tape loops conceived by Lennon. The double album was far from a total disaster: the brilliant Beach Boys pastiche 'Back In The USSR', Harrison's 'While My Guitar Gently Weeps' (on which his friend Eric Clapton plays exceptional lead guitar), McCartney's reggae-influenced 'Ob-La-Di, Ob-La-Da', and Lennon's disturbing 'Happiness Is A Warm Gun' all remain notable. Nonetheless, it was clear that the group, especially Lennon and McCartney, were no longer working in harmony; during the recording of the album Ringo actually left the band, although he rejoined before his departure became common knowledge.

Immediately before the 'double white' album appeared, the first two Beatle solo albums were released on Apple Records. Neither Harrison's *Wonderwall* soundtrack nor *Two Virgins* by Lennon and Yoko possessed a fraction of the mainstream appeal of a Beatles LP. The release of these albums also coincided with Lennon and McCartney growing apart. The next group project was a documentary film about the recording of the new Beatles LP. Although it spawned two timeless new songs, the scheme was abandoned and revived only when the group was in its death throes. One of the classic

---

'As Beatles, we've gone through millions of superficial changes, which mean nothing and haven't changed us. In posh places you get to like avocado and spinach, so you have them every time, and when you've done all that, you can go back. If you feel like cornflakes for lunch, you ask for them.' PAUL

---

hits that did result was 'Get Back', recorded live on the roof of the Apple offices in Savile Row. When the single was released, it credited American keyboard player Billy Preston as special guest, and remained at Number One in Britain and the United States for six and five weeks respectively.

Six weeks later, while 'Get Back' was still in the British top three, 'The Ballad Of John and Yoko', a single credited to The Beatles but actually featuring only Lennon (lead vocals and guitar) and McCartney (piano, drums and backing vocals) entered the UK chart in the top five; as it left the Top Ten in mid-July, it was replaced by 'Give Peace A Chance', the first release by The Plastic Ono Band, effectively the blanket name for most of Lennon's releases until the end of 1972. This single was recorded in a hotel room in Montreal, Canada, where Lennon and his new wife, Yoko, were involved in a 'bed-in' for peace. This publicity-seeking venture involved inviting the world's media to visit them in their hotel room, where they would remain in bed for eight days to raise awareness of their desire for an end to war. By then the crack in the foundations of The Beatles was widening – Lennon, with support from Harrison and Starr, wanted New York lawyer Allen Klein

'John and Yoko? Some people think they're mad, but he's only being John.' RINGO

*'Paul rang me up and said "Look, I'm a bit
fed up with the way things have been going.
Will you come back and produce an album
like you used to ?"'.* GEORGE MARTIN

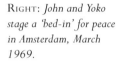

RIGHT: *John and Yoko
stage a 'bed-in' for peace
in Amsterdam, March
1969.*

to be the group's new manager, but McCartney understandably felt that his father-in-law, Lee Eastman, who was also a lawyer, should get the job.

Nevertheless, after the fiasco surrounding the documentary project, the group were contractually obliged to make a new album. George Martin agreed to try to produce the record, as long as it could be recorded at Abbey Road studios, and Abbey Road became the title of the last album recorded by The Beatles. The producer remembered it as 'a very happy album'. With a sleeve picture showing The Beatles on a pedestrian crossing near the studio, the LP was a success, topping the American album chart for eleven weeks and its British equivalent for seventeen; by 1980 it had sold over 10 million copies world-wide.

A distinct return to form after the patchy double LP, *Abbey Road* was also notable for its inclusion of two fine George Harrison songs: 'Something', which was released as a single and became a big hit, and 'Here Comes The Sun', which was later a UK Top Ten hit for Steve Harley. 'Something' was released as another double A-side, coupled with Lennon's magnificently carnal 'Come Together'. Overall, *Abbey Road* was a triumph in a patchy year.

'We tried to put aside all the differences, and although it wasn't an integrated album, because everybody was writing their own material and worked mainly on their own songs, for which the others would reluctantly come in, it was a much happier album than I really expected.'
GEORGE MARTIN (ON THE ABBEY ROAD LP)

'I'm not certain about the songs I've written. Looked at from another person's point of view, as pop songs, I like them, but from my point of view, what I really want to do, I don't like what I've done so far.' GEORGE

'Do I look dead? I'm as fit as a fiddle.'
PAUL ON RUMOURS OF HIS DEATH

...AND FALL

'Paul was telling me the other day that he and I used to have rows about who was the leader. I can't remember them, it had stopped mattering by then. I wasn't so determined to be the leader at all costs. If I did argue, it was just out of pride. All the arguments were just trivial, mainly because we were irritable with working so hard. We were just kids.' JOHN

FACING PAGE: *John and Yoko with their son Sean; family life drew John into a period of musical inactivity.*

THE RESPITE provided by the success of *Abbey Road* was temporary and, sadly, failed to convince The Beatles that their individual ambitions would never match their collective achievements. McCartney's underlying penchant for the melodic and catchy had provided the perfect balance for Lennon's more adventurous but much less civilized tendencies, but separately, their magic lacked consistency. In the absence of anything else (and because he had little choice with the group's two leading lights at loggerheads), Allen Klein decided to hire the celebrated American record producer Phil Spector to salvage the abandoned recordings made during the documentary project. With a working title of 'Get Back' (reflecting the superb chart-topping track recorded on the roof of the Apple building), Spector set about making sense of around thirty hours of material. While he pursued this Herculean task, a new single, 'Let It Be', was released, a classic ballad written by McCartney on which Billy Preston again played keyboards. This instant evergreen was prevented from topping the British chart by actor Lee Marvin mournfully intoning 'Wand'rin' Star', although 'Let It Be' received its just deserts in the United States by reaching Number One, as did 'The Long And Winding Road' a few weeks later. The latter, which was also included on the *Let It Be* album (the fruits of Spector's labours), was not released as a single in Britain, perhaps because Paul McCartney, was unhappy about Spector's unauthorized (by Paul) addition of a full orchestra to a somewhat instrumentally sparse mix; this gave McCartney fresh fuel in his battle with his colleagues over the question of new management, even if the song's commercial success tended to render his complaints rather hollow.

Even before the *Let It Be* album finally emerged in May 1970, McCartney had announced that he had left the group when he became the last of the quartet to release a solo LP. Lennon and Yoko had followed their first experimental LP, *Two Virgins* (which was displayed in shop windows in a

---

'People were robbing us and living off us — £18,000 or £20,000 a week was rolling out of Apple, and nobody was doing anything about it.'

JOHN

---

brown paper bag because it portrayed a naked full frontal view of Mr and Mrs Lennon) with two more equally avant-garde collections, *Life With The Lions* and *The Wedding Album;* the latter was a boxed set containing such valuable items as a photograph of a piece of wedding cake and a copy of their marriage certificate. The Plastic Ono Band had also released two more hit singles, 'Cold Turkey' and 'Instant Karma', and a live LP, *Live Peace In Toronto, 1969,* the first side of which was recognizable as orthodox music and included participation by Eric Clapton. When *Cold Turkey* unexpectedly started to drop down the chart, and in a somewhat ill-advised attempt to boost its flagging sales, Lennon had returned his MBE to Buckingham Palace with a note protesting about British involvement in the Nigerian–Biafran war, British support of American policy in Vietnam, and because 'Cold Turkey' had slipped down the charts. George Harrison's second solo LP was accurately titled *Electronic Sound,* and Ringo's *Sentimental Journey* was a collection of standards.

Perhaps the most interesting of all these early solo efforts was 'Instant Karma', the first track to appear by a Beatle with production by Phil Spector, although there are

'The only thing which is important in life is karma, which roughly means actions. Every action has a reaction, which is equal and opposite.' GEORGE

'Everyone's egos started going crazy. Maybe it was just lack of tact or discretion, but feelings got hurt, and probably the biggest problem of all was that there was no way Yoko Ono or Linda McCartney was going to be in The Beatles.' GEORGE

few clues as to the precise meaning of Lennon's lyrics. However, McCartney's unilateral resignation from the group caused most consternation, among fans and the other Beatles alike, because he insisted on releasing his debut solo album only days before the long-awaited *Let It Be*. In fact, there was little argument from the other

ABOVE: *Paul McCartney's first solo album was released only days before The Beatles' LET IT BE.*

group members about the plain fact that The Beatles were no more, although Paul's announcement led to his being incorrectly regarded as solely responsible for the group's demise. Paul's LP, imaginatively titled *McCartney,* was almost totally a solo effort. An adequate debut, it was arguably preferable to any of the other solo albums by members of the group thus far released, but it was inevitably overshadowed by *Let It Be,* despite the latter's perceived short-comings. The *Let It Be* film also premiered in May 1970, to a predictably cool response, which perhaps was anticipated by the erst-while group members, none of whom both-ered to attend the big night. John and Yoko were already making albums together, and

Paul had made his solo debut. Ringo, the only member of the quartet who was not a songwriter, was the least sure of his artistic survival. However, during the second half of 1970 the drummer was on more Beatle solo albums than any of his colleagues, releasing his own second solo LP, *Beaucoups Of Blues,* a collection of original country and Western songs which he recorded in Nashville. While arguably superior to *Sentimental Journey,* it was still hard work, but because he was also involved in historic projects with Lennon and Harrison, he probably had little time to mourn its commercial failure.

George declared himself happy to be his own boss. His *All Things Must Pass* was an unexpected smash hit: a triple album in a box, it included an enormous hit single, 'My Sweet Lord', the first single by a solo Beatle to top the charts on both sides of the Atlantic, and it topped the American chart for seven weeks, achieving double platinum status. Apart from Ringo, others who played on the triple album included Eric Clapton and the other three musicians who would become Derek and The Dominoes, as well as Klaus Voorman who had befriend-ed The Beatles in Hamburg and was now a respected bass player. Media speculation over possible replacements for McCartney often called Voorman the fifth Beatle, but playing on solo albums by John and George was the closest he got.

Klaus had been in several incarnations of the Plastic Ono Band, including the ad hoc line-up on the live Toronto album and the two recent hit singles, but none of these would attract as much attention as *John Lennon/Plastic Ono Band*, an album often referred to as the 'primal scream LP', on which the faithful Ringo also appeared, and which Phil Spector co-produced. This was not the most accessible album ever made, containing rants by Lennon that were intended to reveal his repressed emotions (as highlighted in psychiatrist Dr Arthur Janov's book *The Primal Scream*, which had deeply impressed John and Yoko).

Each of the four Beatles produced new solo LPs in 1970, and 1971 saw each of them further pursue the directions in which they had embarked. Paul McCartney was the most prolific, exploring the concept of forming a new group, while John Lennon continued to work with Phil Spector and, of course, Yoko Ono. Neither George nor Ringo released a new album during the year, although both enjoyed success in the singles chart, from which Ringo, in particular, had previously been absent as a solo artist.

'When The Beatles split up, I felt on the rocks. I was accused of walking out on them, but I never did. I think we were all pretty weird at the time of the court cases. I'd ring John and he'd tell me not to bother him, and I rang George and what he came out with wasn't Hare Krishna at all.'

PAUL

'If all four of us had to stand up in front of a million fans and they had to line up behind the one they liked best, I think Paul would get most, John and George would be joint second and Ringo would be last.' RINGO

THE SOLO YEARS

'I don't mind if people attack us — because we're so popular, it doesn't matter — but critics can kill records when a lot of people might have enjoyed them. When you're coming up, everyone is all for you, but when you've made it, they want to knock you if they can.' RINGO

FACING PAGE: *Ringo Starr in* THE MAGIC CHRISTIAN *— 'I used to get offered film parts just because I was an ex-Beatle ...'*

PAUL MCCARTNEY's debut solo single, 'Another Day', was also his first hit 45, reaching the Top Ten on both sides of the Atlantic just after George Harrison's 'My Sweet Lord' had peaked. As Paul's hit dropped down the chart, a new Plastic Ono Band single, 'Power To The People', passed it going in the opposite direction, and then came Ringo's first hit single, 'It Don't Come Easy', which he also wrote. Four Top Ten singles by members of The Beatles made it seem almost like the Sixties, although the rest of 1971 brought Seventies reality. Ringo played the part of Frank Zappa in Zappa's *200 Motels* movie, in which Zappa confusingly also appeared as himself and Keith Moon of The Who played the part of a nun (!). George, who was increasingly drawn towards the music and culture of the Indian subcontinent, staged a massive all-star benefit concert in New York to raise money for Bangladesh, then a province in Pakistan where many people were dying of starvation during a civil war. Artistically, the Concert For Bangladesh was a huge success, although neither McCartney nor Lennon performed. Lennon reportedly refused to appear without Yoko, while Paul supposedly made it a condition of his appearance that George must agree to dis-solve The Beatles' partnership, which was a bone of contention at the time.

Paul's lawyers had taken the rest of the group to court, and a receiver had been appointed, but the impact of this victory had been lessened when it was revealed that Klein had earned 44 million dollars for The Beatles during 1970. While all this was unfolding, Paul released a second solo LP, *Ram,* using session musicians from New York, one of whom, drummer Denny Seiwell, would subsequently join Wings, the new band launched by the McCartneys. Two of the songs on *Ram,* 'Too Many People' and 'Dear Boy', were interpreted by Lennon as criticism from his ex-partner.

When Lennon's next solo LP, *Imagine,* appeared, it not only included 'How Do You Sleep', a bitter song seemingly responding to Paul's supposed complaints, and the more pitying 'Crippled Inside', but also 'Imagine', the title track, which is regarded as Lennon's most inspired and enduring solo composition. *Imagine* was the Lennon album his fans had been patiently awaiting and is widely viewed as his finest solo collection.

The same could not be said of Paul McCartney's second LP of the year, *Wild Life,* the first album by Wings, the group he

RIGHT: *At the end of
1972 Ringo made his
debut as a film director
with* BORN TO BOOGIE.

would lead throughout the decade. *Wild Life*
certainly wasn't a triumph, nor was it a disaster (although it was the only original
McCartney album before 1979 that failed to
reach the top three of the American chart
and the Top Ten of the British chart).

Although 1972 started as George's year,
with the release of a second boxed triple LP
– the recording of his 'Concert for
Bangladesh' – his good intentions were
undermined when the US Internal Revenue
Service insisted on tax revenues from
the release, causing a delay in the much-
needed cash reaching the beleaguered
people of Bangladesh, for whose benefit the
concert had been staged, and who were
dying of starvation. Nevertheless, the boxed
set topped the UK chart and won a
Grammy Award, and George's karma was
intact, as he had acted throughout in good
faith. He and Ravi Shankar (his sitar teacher)
accepted a UNICEF award for their fund-
raising efforts.

Ringo also enjoyed a satisfactory year,
releasing his second Top Ten single, 'Back
Off Boogaloo', which again highlighted his
improvement as a songwriter. He had
appeared in a non-musical role in a
'spaghetti Western', *Blindman*, premiered at
the end of 1971, and at the end of 1972

made his debut as a film director with *Born To Boogie,* essentially a concert documentary about teeny-bop star Marc Bolan.

The most active ex-Beatle was Paul, who released three singles during the year, two of which were banned by the BBC, although all three became hits (albeit smaller than had been expected). The first one, 'Give Ireland Back To The Irish', was the first Wings release on which lead guitarist Henry McCullough (ex-The Grease Band, Joe Cocker's early backing group) played, but the political naiveté displayed in the song title obviously provoked controversy. Perhaps that was why Paul's follow-up was the nursery rhyme, 'Mary Had A Little Lamb', which stood little chance of being banned, but only just reached the US top thirty because many people refused to take it seriously. The end of the year brought 'Hi Hi Hi' / 'C Moon', the former being banned for being sexually suggestive. McCartney became the first group member to return to touring, as Wings played tours of Britain and later, Europe. He was also charged with drug offences twice during the year, first with possession of cannabis during the Scandinavian leg of the European tour, and then with cultivation of marijuana at his Scottish farm.

John Lennon spent much of the year in political activism, and in trying to avoid being deported from the United States, where he had been living since September 1971. After taking part in a demonstration in New York in support of a boycott of British exports in protest against the British government's political stance over Northern Ireland he was regarded in American government circles as an undesirable alien, and in March was the subject of a deportation order that cited his 1968 conviction for drug possession. John appealed against the order in March 1973.

The only single released by the Lennons in 1972 in Britain was a seasonal item, 'Happy Xmas (War Is Over)', which had actually been recorded and released in the US at the end of 1971, but could not appear in Britain at that time due to a dispute over songwriting credits. An obvious Yuletide classic, it was produced by Phil Spector, and was a UK hit during no less than six Christmas periods between 1972 and 1988. Of far less note was a double album titled *Some Time In New York City,* a sprawling mess comprising half studio recordings and half live recordings, some from a London show in 1969, and the rest from a New York show with Frank Zappa's Mothers of

FACING PAGE: *Togetherness – John and Yoko in New York during the 1970s.*

'Having just celebrated our fourth wedding anniversary, we are not prepared to sleep in separate beds.' JOHN

'Don't you think it's time to end all this silliness and give John his visa? He's one of the greatest, and America should be proud that John wants to live here.'

RINGO ON US MOVES TO DEPORT JOHN

Invention, including two undistinguished compositions entitled 'Jamrag' and 'Scumbag'. To call 1972 a disappointing year for the four ex-Beatles was almost an understatement, and the next year would inevitably produce work of greater merit.

For Paul McCartney 1973 was a brilliant year, during which he released two albums, one of which is generally regarded as his best ever. One significant difference was that whereas his last three singles and the *Wild Life* album had been credited simply to Wings, most of his 1973 releases gave the name of the act as Paul McCartney and Wings. The first of these was an impressive ballad, *My Love,* which topped the US chart and sold a million copies. It was included on *Red Rose Speedway,* the first of the albums, which also reached Number One in the United States. In June, Paul's theme to the James Bond movie *Live And Let Die* was a Top Ten hit on both sides of the Atlantic but soon afterwards both Henry McCullough and Denny Seiwell left Wings. The remaining trio of Paul, Linda and Denny Laine flew to Nigeria to record a new LP, *Band On The Run,* which was widely acclaimed after its release at the end of the year and topped the charts all over the world, remaining in the US lists for well over two years and exceeding 6 million sales by the end of 1974.

The other ex-Beatles were, unsurprisingly, unable to match this success, yet each of the three enjoyed a modicum of success during the year. George made Number One with both a single, 'Give Me Love (Give Me Peace On Earth)', and the LP from which it was excerpted, *Living In The Material World,* but it was clear that his mind was more on spiritual matters than on music. John Lennon proceeded along his path of self-discovery (or self-indulgence, as many critics regarded it), and Ringo not only wrote and scored a big hit with a third single in three years, 'Photograph' (which was his first US Number One as a solo artist), but also appeared in a major role in a highly rated feature film, *That'll Be The Day,* starring David Essex. However, the best news of the year for the quartet came when Allen Klein's contract with The Beatles ended and was not renewed.

LEFT: *While touring in 1974, George said, 'I don't care if nobody comes to see me … I'm going to do what I feel within myself.'*

'Ghandi says create and preserve the image of your choice. The image of my choice is not Beatle George – those who want that can go and see Wings. Why live in the past? Be here now.'

GEORGE

DEATH AND REBIRTH

'I always felt, as did millions of other people, that it would be a wonderful thing which we would all love to see happen. It would have been the greatest, the ultimate thrill for any producer on the planet.'

RICHARD PERRY (PRODUCER OF THE RINGO ALBUM), ON A BEATLES REUNION

FACING PAGE: *Ringo Starr and his All-Starr Band — 'with this band there was a really magical atmosphere'.*

RINGO STARR enjoyed his most productive and successful period as a solo artist in 1973/4, with the release of his third solo LP, *Ringo*. In fact, the *Ringo* LP involved each of the four ex-Beatles. When George Harrison, who had played on all Ringo's hit singles, was in Los Angeles working on the *Ringo* LP, John Lennon also dropped in to the studio to hear the completed material, and as well as contributing 'I'm The Greatest', a song he had written for and about Ringo, played piano on the track. During the period when the album was being assembled, producer Richard Perry was working with Paul McCartney on a separate project, and Paul gave Perry a track titled 'Six O'clock', which he and Linda had recorded, to which Ringo added a lead vocal. Perry went on to produce Ringo's 1974 LP, *Goodnight Vienna,* which also went gold and included two more US Top Ten singles, 'Only You' (another oldie) and 'No No Song'. The *Goodnight Vienna* title track was written by John Lennon, and 'Snookeroo' was donated by Elton John and Bernie Taupin.

Apart from his work with Ringo, George Harrison launched his own record label, Dark Horse, and also embarked on a disastrous US tour, which was savaged by critics. Harrison was pursuing his fascination with India, and was on the verge of losing his wife, Patti Boyd, to his friend, Eric Clapton, who was in love with Patti. In 1976, a court in America ruled that Harrison's 'My Sweet Lord' plagiarized 'He's So Fine', a 1963 hit by US girl group The Chiffons (although George maintained that if anything, his song had been inspired by the 1969 hit by the Edwin Hawkins Singers, 'Oh Happy Day'), and the publishers of 'He's So Fine' were awarded damages of over half a million dollars.

John Lennon was also experiencing marital problems. He had separated from Yoko, who had seemingly encouraged him to take an extended Californian holiday with her personal assistant, May Pang. For almost a year John and Yoko were on opposite coasts of America while John and May were an item around Hollywood.

John's 1973 LP, *Mind Games,* had been only a moderate success, and its title track when released as a single had only just reached the US top twenty, which led to suggestions that he was on the skids. Although it was some improvement on *Some Time In New York City,* and was supposedly an attempt to return to the more acceptable commercial style of *Imagine,* the *Mind Games* album had included a silent track, 'Nutopian National Anthem', as well as a printed 'Declaration of Nutopia', apparently a conceptual country with no land, no boundaries, no passports (clearly a reference to the deportation order against which Lennon was fighting), no people and no laws (other than cosmic). The *Walls And Bridges* LP, which rivalled *Imagine* in topping the US album chart, included US Top Ten single, '#9 Dream' (rather better than 'Revolution 9', fortunately) and 'Whatever Gets You Thru The Night'.

Elton John had played on John's 'Whatever Gets You Thru The Night' single, and had made Lennon promise to appear on-stage with him if the single topped the US chart. It did, so Lennon was the surprise guest at Elton's Madison Square Garden show. Yoko was in the audience; she and John met face to face and within a few weeks were reunited.

During his stay in Los Angeles John had started preparing an album of his favourite rock 'n' roll oldies, working with Phil Spector. However, as Lennon was in a strange frame of mind, the results were unsatisfactory. Spector took away the tapes and refused all Lennon's attempts to retrieve them until late 1974, when Lennon embarked on a week of intensive recording sessions to complete the album, although its release was delayed until early 1975, as *Walls And Bridges* was still selling well. Titled *Rock 'n' Roll,* the oldies collection would be Lennon's last album of new recordings for more than five years. His reconciliation with Yoko had resulted in her becoming pregnant. When Sean Ono Lennon was born on 9 October 1975, John vowed to spend the first five years of Sean's life being a model father, and while few believed he would stick to his words, Lennon effectively disappeared until 1980. While he busied himself as one of the highest profile 'house husbands' of all time, he left business matters to his wife. Yoko's inspired investment programme ensured that the Lennons were not merely financially solvent, but became multi-millionaires.

'Yoko and I have basically decided to be with our baby as much as we can until we feel we can take time off to create things outside the family.'

JOHN

RIGHT: *George Harrison and his second wife, Olivia, with whom he seemed to finally find fulfilment.*

George Harrison seemed to flounder in musical terms, but developed a new interest in the cinema through Hand Made Films. George also remarried, and when the second Mrs Harrison, Olivia Arias, gave birth to a son, Dhani, in October 1978, it seemed that George was finally secure, happy and fulfilled.

'*The man who offered us five million dollars each to reform supposedly also wanted to promote a fight between a man and a shark. My suggestion was that he fight the shark and the winner could promote a Beatles concert.*'

GEORGE ON A PROPOSED BEATLES REUNION

And what of Paul McCartney? Various members joined and left Wings, and the hit albums continued: 1975's *Venus And Mars,* 1976's *Wings At The Speed Of Sound* and the same year's *Wings Over America,* a live triple LP, all topped the US chart. At the same time Paul also accumulated more huge hit

LEFT: *Paul and Linda McCartney have stayed together despite often fierce public criticism.*

singles: 1976's 'Silly Love Songs' sold a million copies, 1977's bagpipe-powered 'Mull Of Kintyre' topped the UK chart for nine weeks (but was completely ignored in the US) and 1978's 'With A Little Luck' was another US chart-topper, his sixth as a solo artist. At the start of 1980 Paul was arrested in Tokyo for possession of marijuana and spent several days in prison. This brush with authority obviously had not affected his popularity in the US, the biggest world market, as in June he was back at the top of the US singles chart with a live version of 'Coming Up', a song that had been included on his second solo album, *McCartney II,* which was also released in 1980. By the start of that new decade Paul was the ex-Beatle with the most consistent track record by far. Ringo's purple period was effectively over and George spent many months in the last years of the decade following a new hobby, Grand Prix motor-racing, releasing only one original LP between 1976 and 1981.

However, neither George's self-imposed silence nor Ringo's unsurprising artistic decline caused as much interest as John Lennon's disappearance from view, because both Harrison and Starr remained periodically visible. When he did return to public life at the end of his five year 'exile' in New York's exclusive apartment block, the Dakota Building, he was quick to explain that he had not been twiddling his thumbs for five years; among other things, he had learned how to cook. In October 1980

'I've mastered the art of rice — they say anyone can cook rice, but few people cook it well. I cook it reasonably well. I can do fish and I've learned to make bread, which I was thrilled with. I took a Polaroid of my first bread.'

JOHN ON HIS COOKING SKILLS

Lennon released his first new record since February 1975, '(Just Like) Starting Over', which became a hit all over the world, although critics were generally dismissive, due to its rather bland qualities. It was followed in November by an album, *Double Fantasy,* which was similarly regarded. The general view appeared to be that while it was obviously a good thing that Lennon was back in action, his overlong lay-off had

LEFT: *John came to feel at home in New York; to him, the public always seemed friendly and honestly interested in his life.*

'*I would be walking around tense, waiting for somebody to say something or jump on me, and it took me two years to unwind. I can go right out of this door now and go in a restaurant or to the movies — you want to know how great that is?*'

JOHN

blunted the abrasive qualities that had made him great. Both the single and the LP on which it was included seemed to have peaked in the British charts by early December, and were on the way down, until the ultimate tragedy for Beatle fans occurred: John Lennon was murdered. Mark Chapman was a so-called fan who had asked Lennon for his autograph a little while before. On a second brief encounter with the ex-Beatle outside the Dakota building he pumped five bullets into Lennon for no obvious reason.

As both '(Just Like) Starting Over' and the *Double Fantasy* album began to sell incredibly swiftly in the wake of the tragedy, both topping charts all over the planet, the world caught its breath, perhaps reflecting on John's earlier pronouncement on the advantages of living in New York. The other ex-Beatles were understandably alarmed at such a motiveless murder.

It was the end of an era. No more would Paul, George and Ringo have to tolerate the question they had been asked so frequently – when are The Beatles going to reunite and make another album? The Beatles were the greatest rock group the world may ever see. Their appeal has yet to be approached, let alone exceeded.

'John's shooting definitely scared all three of us — when a fan recognizes me and rushes over, it definitely makes me nervous.' GEORGE

'When we came out of the Dakota building, I didn't need to hear people telling me how much they loved The Beatles. I was there to see my friend.' RINGO

'I don't like being the careful one of The Beatles, I'd rather be immediate like John. He was all action, the loudest in any crowd, but he could be a manoeuvring swine, which no one ever realized. Now since his death, he's become Martin Luther Lennon, but that wasn't him either, he wasn't some sort of holy saint.' PAUL